THE FIGHT WITHIN

LOVE MARIE HOBBS

Copyright © 2021 Love Marie Hobbs All rights reserved.

COPYRIGHT

Table of Contents

INTRODUCTION IV

CHAPTER 1 1

CHAPTER 2 3

CHAPTER 3 7

CHAPTER 4 11

CHAPTER 5 16

CHAPTER 6 21

CHAPTER 7...26

PRAYER 33

ABOUT THE AUTHOR 34

INTRODUCTION

Depression is often related to feeling hopeless. More than 264 million people deal with this mood disorder. It is no friend to anyone. Have you or anyone ever been depressed? If so, this guide will lead you into a place of freedom. Depressions tight grip will have to lose your life.

Take a step and turn the page you will be equipped to live a vibrant life again. You will be able to put Depression down and pick-up hope. It is not over for you. You do matter and this does not have to be a fatality. This is a new beginning for you.

Depression does not have to win. You can win and overcome. You are an overcomer. You are not hopeless there is still hope for you. This is not the end of your life what happened. This guide will allow you to be able to stand on your two feet again and live.

Turn the page and let us defeat this enemy together.

CHAPTER 1

What is depression so many people talk about it? It is often mentioned in every household, church, even in schools.

Depression is simply a mood disorder that causes a persistent feeling of sadness and loss of interest.

It is just plain feeling hopeless. It feels as though life is over. That life without you would be a better place.

I am here to let you know that is not true. Life is so much better because you are in it.

Depression has crept its way in many homes uninvited. Depression does not introduce itself. It bombards the mind without warning.

Depression is not vital to the mind. It is detrimental to your health. Depression smoothers the life out of you slowly. It has no substance Depression leaves you empty.

Depression is dark, gloomy, cold.

This toxic trait is mind-blowing that wants you to blow out your brains. Depression lies it never tells the truth. Depression is tantalizing. It is not friendly it is often rude.

Depression comes to steal kill and destroy.

Who can overcome this deadly blow? Who can survive the treacherous being? Who can survive when surrounded by death? Who can?

That person is you the fight within Can be silenced and that is the Key.

CHAPTER 2

Depression comes in a person's life when they are doing well. I wonder why that is? Well, just think about it would depression show up when you are doing badly? No, it starts at the peak of your life when it is going good. This allows depression to have a fatal sting. It comes when you are celebrating. This allows the celebrating to feel like it is a mistake.

Have you ever been celebrating and suddenly, a sadness tries to overtake you? This may happen because the people you want to celebrate with you are not there. So now you start to feel hopeless because you feel like you were not good enough for them to come.

In addition, to being celebrated, you cannot get past the thought of rejection. Depression comes to rob you when starting a business, it seems like nobody likes your product. This causes you to feel singled out.

Ironically, you can be selling the same thing as someone else. But no one buys from you. That sends the seller with thoughts of giving up if you are not careful.

A person gets depressed because depression is comfort.

Although, it is a place of continuous sadness it is a place to find security. Depression comes like a thief in the night. Depression is often lead by a tragedy or series of hurts. It grows with every thought that plays in your mind.

That is why every thought we think is not always a good thought. Our mind is the biggest battlefield. There is a fight there every day just trying to do what is right.

When your mind has been drenched with depression it causes thinking to minimize. It is hard to even get a clear thought out. The only thoughts that feed the brain are the negative ones.

Depression is also caused by weight gain or weight loss. It steals confidence and causes you to feel like you are the ugliest thing on God's green earth. When that is never the case everything God made is beautiful and that means you.

Death is a full trigger for depression. Any type of loss makes you feel hopeless. It is often a place where you can never overcome that hole that is in the heart. It is a fatal sting that lingers around by the second.

Depression creeps in the schools. Kids already expect some parents and if they do not meet it. They become depressed trying to be someone there not.

Moreover, they hide so much even from themselves. The fact that they may not even want to go to college. Depression can just appear in our lives or it can be projected on a person.

I know you never looked at it like that. How many times have you become depressed because of the actions of a decision of others? I know I have many times than one.

That came and wholeheartedly sucked the natural life out of me.

Depression is dangerous those are some waters you do not want to mingle in. The longer you let your feet get wet the sooner you jump in the water.

Depression comes at any given time it does not prepare you for its entrance.

Momentarily, depression does not even feel like depression at times. Just think of this global pandemic. It is a stay home order for most, so you stay home. You just enjoy your days. Not realizing you are eating more.

Starving from social companionship. It seems like nothing is good on tv. Every book has been read twice. So now you are running out of options. But at the same time, you run out of strength. Your countenance changes. Once happy now you are grumpy. You are so groggy and even though you are already socially distancing. You want to distance yourself more.

Now, do you see how depression crept up on you unaware? It seems like it is right. But it has the wrong intentions.

CHAPTER 3

Depression does not have a certain person it targets. So do not believe the myths that say it is in the poor homes, amongst a certain race, a certain social status. Those are all lies depression, unfortunately, has no respect for persons.

Depression can happen to anybody at any given time. depression can target a small child and the oldest adult. It can come in the black home, caucasian home mexican home. It does need you to give it the address it knows how to make its way home.

Depression starts and does not finish until it has caused havoc.

Just think of a vibrant child enjoying life. So, suddenly, the behavior changes. Often, we as parents overlook it because we believe kids have no care in the world.

Generally, that would be the case. What about the peer pressure out there? Sex is displayed like it is the next top model.

It is hard to keep purity in these times especially for a child. If they do not give in. Then they must deal with being called lame a square. It is easy for us as parents to say get over it. But we are not the ones that have to face these taunting words every day. In some cases, they may be getting bullied. It wears and tears on a person's mental state. once again that is where depression forms in the mind.

If a child is having trouble processing their thoughts, they become depressed.

I am not judging the parents we often look past the behavior because we are so busy with life. We do not see the changes in the mood swings of the sunken eyes. We just say things as they teenagers. that is how they are. Well, I am here to tell you that is not how they are teenagers should not want to end Life.

It is so easy for depression to hide because we do not expose his ammunition. It is always labeled as something else. It is never held in high regard it is swept under the rug. I know I have overlooked things when my kids have been depressed.

I am just bringing awareness to end this vicious cycle.

In adults, the same thing occurs it is swept under the rug. oftentimes telling a person to be strong is just the new norm. It is the cliche of today. It seems like some great advice. But what if they have no strength to even make it through the next moment? So our words must be fruitful or less.

Listening to a person can be a great way to allow them to find a safe place in you.

Depression does not care if you are rich. You can have all the money in the world and still be depressed. Just look at all the ones that took their lives. Money was unable to sustain them.

See Depression does not always look hopeless these people had smiles that could light up a room. But was being lit on fire on the inside. It is true depression comes to sweep you off your feet. It is not satisfied till you are laying on your back in a church. You can defeat depression it does not matter your race gender social status. There is still hope for you.

It does not end on this page keep reading your breakthrough is almost there.

Keep believing that you will overcome this. The next page can change your life.

You came this far keep going. Nothing is too hard for God.

CHAPTER 4

In some cases, Depression is mild. While other cases are severe. I had Depression for three long years once a small, framed woman turned into a full figure woman in months. I was often distant. I had no emotional empathy. I was still on the inside nothing was going out. Nothing could get in. I was surrounded by people, but I was still alone. The aloneness on the inside consumed my outer shell.

I daydreamed to find a space to occupy. I was snatched off my feet dangling amid nowhere.

Depression came for its finality wanting me to lose my mind. See depression was ready for the kill literally. It never gave up on its assignment. See depression persevered through the mask I wore. It hijacked my joy.

Depression was my master, and I was following depressions every command.

See depression baits you in and throws you off an cliff. It rearranges the bullets in the gun depression stinks.

Depression has no time frame it can go away in a week. Without the right tools it can last a lifetime.

Those three years of my life were a living nightmare.

I could not get past the front door. Let alone explore the full house. Depression had me stuck.

I know you can relate to what I am saying. I want you to know you are not alone. There is still a new day for you. You are not a failure. Losing a job, closing your business, losing a mate is not the end of the world. You may say I wish that were the case. I just lost my loved one love. I know death is the ultimate sting. Even to that you can overcome that place. God will heal every place you hurt. You may say I am mad at God. That is why I have my depression. I want you to know in life we blame God for everything in the world. Never realizing there is the Devil and our own conscious. It is so easy to blame God because he did not do as we said.

Meaning I prayed for it did not happen. That is not faith receiving everything you ask for. faith is believing that God heard me, and he is answering my prayer. No wait not yet or I have something better. If we realized all the things God has kept us from. And the doors we wanted open so bad you soon are relieved that door stayed shut.

That relationship did not work out, so you soon find out why. Where you were once depressed you now see it was a blessing in disguise.

See God protected you. God gave you a way of escape when the rejection hit. I know I am not the only one that can vouch for these situations.

It is real these very things can send us in a depression frenzy. What depression triggers is the Loss. Depression Maximizes the offense, loss and minimizes God. If God loved, you why are you going through if God heard you why you still not married? Why you still broke?

If God loves you so much why he let them die? The devil is crafty and if we are not careful, he will fool us and win.

See he always makes the problem boisterous so you can blame God. The very person you gone need to get through the storm. He wants you to not trust.

However, when he is planting seed of doubt you are losing. The more he can keep you from God the better chance he has of his victory.

Just think of the times you may have thought about suicide or attempted it. Who do you think sent that neighbor over? Or had a tv show just randomly pop on that said do not do it. Better yet in my case a person sends a random text come outside.

That is God the devil is not gone have nobody come and intervened he wanted to claim your soul, but God said no.

It was the very person he wanted you to give up.

All Good and perfect gifts come from above.

Life, safety, and peace are gifts from God above.

So, the next time you are visited by those haunting thoughts remember it was God that kept you another day. It was God that gave your life.

It was God that loves you. although these things happen you can live another day. They may have left you God is just making room for the right people to walk in your life. See nobody can leave your life and God not replace them with better.

It may not even be a bad situation God may be transitioning you to a better place.

All business starts off slow unless your family is already established and rich. I believe this happens so you can appreciate the first dollar you made. As well as the first thousand you made. So, no it is not the end for you. You have a purpose on earth that only you can fulfill. The first purpose is to live another day.

CHAPTER 5

Simultaneously, we have pointed out depression. It has taking over the minds of 264 million people. That is truly insane that is why it is so important to come out of this place. Now you may say love I do not feel depressed I want to give you what form it comes in.

Symptoms of Depression

- Feelings of constant sadness

- Loss of interest, hobbies, sports, family functions, even sexual desire.

- Weight gain, rapid weight loss.

- Sleep disruption, too much sleep not enough sleep insomnia

- Trouble thinking

- Feeling Hopeless

- Recurring headaches, muscle pain (mainly in the back)

- Frequent thoughts of death.

- Suicidal thoughts or attempts.

If you have any of these symptoms you may be dealing with depression. These symptoms come and go so do not be fooled by that.

Joseph in the bible was probably extremely depressed the bible does not talk about it. But I can only imagine how he felt just seventeen at the time. Then he was sold into slavery, being away from home, no family.

Not to mention, he was falsely accused of rape and thrown in jail.

So, you see in the bible Joseph was once thriving then his world got turned upside down.

This may have happened to you. Now, you posses one or maybe all these symptoms you really have no idea how you got here.

Wanting to engage in social activities but it seems like everyone can see your failures. It is like you holding up a sign that says ''I Am Worthless''.

Depression causes you to isolate from people also. Now at time fasting from people is good. But you can identify when it is unhealthy. It starts to take over your whole life.

Isolation has been mistaken as a safe haven. It is a death sentence.

Have you notice when being alone the thoughts are potent?

It seems like it is one negative thought after another.

Ironically, it just happens out the blue. You talking to a person then you start to get angry. sad or very quiet.

Yes, these are also signs of depression.

Depression also comes through a Doctor report.

It makes you feel hopeless. Depression tells you are going to die. I know for me having severe sickness for 12 years. That is where most of my depression lies. I felt like a leper in the bible.

Sickness for me was shame based. Who can relate to that feeling? For many days I was like Lord you got to do something. And honestly at times it felt like he left. But that was never the case Hebrews 13: 15 "He promised me he would never leave me or forsake me'. He did just that. He stayed by my side through it all. Just like he is by your side.

He has never left you and he never will. You are not alone although it gets lonely. He can comfort all that pain you are holding on to yes. Yes, that pain from Molestation, that pain from rejection, that pain from loss, yes that pain of not feeling adequate.

Believe it or not depression always has a root it is triggered by something tragic or even just a small breakup. And grows into something big.

See how that works all the; lies he tells you. It is so easy for us to believe were ugly fat than to believe were beautiful or handsome. Because your minds are prone to bad thoughts. Have you even told somebody you are getting married or starting a business or having a child? They never say congratulations. Its first a negative response Oh you sure you ready? For instance, this can cause you to second guess your decision. That is what depression does it causes you to second guess God existence in your life.

Depression does not play fair. In order to defeat this demon, you must get ready to go to war. Are you ready to get rid of depression once and for all?

Are you ready to live again?

I do not hear you? Are you ready to put depression under your feet and out of your mind? I cannot hear you are you ready. Say with me I am ready. I am ready. Then let us turn the next page and be ready to get rid of this ugly disorder that has consumed your life. Let us get ready. Do you have your tools? That is right you do not you do not know how to defeat it.

Right, that is why the next page is the next level. Follow me as I follow Christ.

CHAPTER 6

Overcoming something simply means that you gain control of the problem or situation that was supposed to control you. Now how do you overcome something so devastated I am glad you ask.

Okay lets sit down let us take notes and strategize. Because we're about to go somewhere. You still with me. Let us keep going you are almost at the finish line. That blow you took should have knocked you out.

But I am here with some spiritual food that will carry you the rest of the way. I know you thirsty you have been fighting a lifetime it may seems. I am going to introduce you to the living water.

Basically. you will never thirst again. I know you got bruises and scars. But this next chapter in life it will seem as though you have never been in the ring.

Let us fight in the Spirt. Fighting this thing physically almost got you knocked.

Out now I hear you say love I do not know how to fight. Let alone fight in the Spirt.

I get it that is why God is gone fight for you. you just got to follow the lead and come out and walk over the troubled waters.

So again, are you ready? Let me hear you say "I am ready to be free". "I am more than enough". "Depression will not defeat me".

"I will defeat it". "My life is not over today is a new beginning". How did that feel? Can you feel those affirmations going through your veins? That is the seed of life.

Now repeat after me "I am fearfully and wonderfully made". God did not make a mistake when he made me. I cannot hear you. "I am the head and not the tail". "I am more than a conqueror in Christ Jesus". "I am the apple of God eye".

Oh, my that means you are all that and some. You are a Queen you are a King. that means that you are pretty darn special. This means you are precious to God. Wow can you imagine if you had of been the only person on earth. Jesus would have died and rose just for you. Say with me "I am worth it".

Okay you ready now I feel the adrenaline boiling time to knock Depression out.

So, this generational cycle will leave you and your family.

Now you know depression is tough so it will not go down without a fight. But you got this look around you cannot see them, but God has called angels to help you in the fight.

Psalm 91:11 11 For he will command his angels concerning you to guard you in all your ways.

So, you got back up so stay focused you have been in the ring long enough. It is time to get that championship belt.

Now Depression has called his boys. Do not fear see molestation, grief, loss, and rejection. They been knocked out before by the Blood of Jesus. So, they got to go down again,

Now as you stand outside the ring you see your opponents; they look scary I know. But look at molestation it was not your fault so let us clear the air. It happened to the best of us. You are not a mistake and you will have the love you desire in life. A man/woman will love and cherish and honor you.

They will not see you as a piece of meat they will see you as a reward God has given them.

You do not have to lay on your back to be accepted you can stand on your two feet and walk the aisle to your love. Oh yes baby it is still hope. God can change your gloomy days to a joyous ray of light. Get ready.

See molestation is crafty it wants you to hate not to forgive and be bitter. See those are those emotions where you feel that rage. That they hurt me, so I want to see them hurt. Get ready for molestation to lose its power.

What if I told you unforgiveness will keep you in prison? But forgiveness will set you free. Now do you want to be free today? Say it with me "I will be free from my past it will no longer hold me in bondage".

Now we have grief creeping up. It leaves you hopeless and full of despair. What if I told you if you let God in, he can comfort that hurt? The very hurt you clinging onto he can get rid of. Now when you think of your loved one or that broken relationship differently.

You will be able to hold on to the memories and smile of the good.

Now you may say love I have no good memories that may be the case.

God gone give you brand new thoughts you will be released from grief deadly grip. It is watching you like a hawk. It does not want to let go but it has too today and the days to come.

Sickness comes with shame and guilt. How did this happen to me? Why wasn't I eating right? I am going to die? I feel like a leper.

Sickness brings all that to the ring. Do not be dismayed even that can be put on its back. Are you ready to go to war?

If so, turn the page one more time and LET'S FIGHT.

CHAPTER 7

Now you see the opponents you know what they are capable of that is good. Now you got to show them who is in control.

Depression cannot thrive where it has no thoughts. So, let us get the mind right first then the body will follow,

Romans 12:2 "And be not conformed to this world: but be ye transformed by the renewing of your mind, that ye may prove what is that good, and acceptable, and perfect, will of God."

I told you God has a perfect will for your life you are not a mistake.

Renewing the mind consist of reading the bible. Also, Books that will up lift and encourage. And daily affirmations that will soothe the mind.

First, you must believe what you are reading. You must exchange those negative thoughts with what God says about you.

You can find that in the bible. As you read and study you will see that you are not alone. Some of the ones in the bible have been through worse than you could ever imagine. God brought them out. Look at Daniel being thrown in the Lion's Den.

Yikes, that is enough to be scared depressed about but because he knew God, he was able to use the lion as a pillow. That is the same with you. Your going to be able to lay on your problems like a pillow.

You can read that in Daniel 6 and you will see how Daniels enemies were dealt with.

Just like those enemies that are staring at you from the other side of the ring. You gone be able to lay on them as a pillow.

Second, prayer is what you need to do. Prayer causes us to be in the presence of God. And anytime anything encounters Jesus their life will never be the same. The more time you spend in prayer and reading the word the more you will be transformed.

For instance, if my mind is occupied with what God says about me, I have no time to believe what the devil says about me.

God is renewing your mind and changing your life at the same time.

God is amazing. Can you see how these to have to go hand in hand. You cannot have one without the other. God is so good.

Now this is a process so keep going do not give up. Because you have made your mind to be free. Depression will try harder.

Depression may even bring the ex around to make you think it will work. RUN. I know God can restore marriages even relationships. But until you are healed. Keep moving it is the trigger of the enemy. They are still going to do the same this time it will be intense what they do.

Depression will make it seem like you are moving forward but you are taking steps back as you take your ex back.

Seriously flee 1 Thessalonians 5:22. Reject every kind of evil.

If God has not changed their heart the devil still has it be wise.

Third, forgive yourself no longer hold on to guilt and shame. It happened you cannot do anything about it.

The things are this God knows are life already.

We are just acting it out.

We can choose what character we want to be meaning. How you navigate through life is up to you. Now some things we can rush in life. But understand God still has the story written. He knows what is gone happen before it does. He knows the beginning from the end. He knows what will happen in this life we do not.

Knowing this gives me hope it allows me to understand nothing gets past God and if it happened it was a reason. Whether it is good or bad. Even the devil must get permission from God. Because our lives already have an end. Today I want you to know God has a fruitful end for you if you do not give up. Today is the day to get up not give up.

However, you have come to far to give up now. You still got breathe in your body you still have purpose.

- My body is healthy; my mind is brilliant; my soul is tranquil.

- If I can change my thoughts, I can change anything.

- I not a mistake.

- I have purpose.

- To love myself, is to fully love.

- I do not need anybody's approval but my own.

- I am more than enough.

- I am forgiven.

- Jesus Loves me.

- I am not the product of my past.

- I am an overcomer.

- I am not a victim I am victorious.

- I will achieve great things with small steps.

- I am not a failure.

- My mind and my heart will remain open today.

- I can love again.

- I am vibrant.

- The world is a great place because I am in it.

- God uniquely designed me handcrafted in love.

You shall recover it all you have used these tools and guess what look. Your accusers are gone. Those thoughts are starting to leave you are on your way to a brand-new life. Look at the ring where is depression and his army now defeated. If you stay on this path you will not go wrong. Jesus is your hope today with him you will win, win, win.

Also, you will need to listen to anointed Christian music. This will change the atmosphere and soothe your soul and mind. Ask God to lead you to the church or online services. These will help you grow, be inspired, empower, and encourage you on your journey. In the presence of God there is a great exchange. The more you give to him the more he supplies..

Now if you have never accepted Jesus as a personal Lord and savior. Today is the day tomorrow is not promised to any of us.

Today is the day you be redeemed from sin and live a life that guarantees you joy, peace and love. it does not exempt trouble, but you got the tools you need to rise above the trouble.

Confess with your mouth that Jesus is Lord he is the Son of God sent by God to cleanse the sins of the world. If you believe in your heart that God raised him from the dead.

He is the savior and not just a prophet you shall be saved. You got the tools to be on your way.

if will have bumps roadblocks but Jesus will allow you to overcome. you are overcoming Depression you can overcome anything. God loves You He has you in the Palm of his hand.

Be blessed and know this too shall pass.

PRAYER

Father God,

I pray in the name of Jesus that you heal the mind of the person reading this. Let them know their struggle has a solution. That you are willing to comfort the mind and heart. that nothing is too hard for them Let them Know you can heal everywhere pain rest. That during this you can give them a peace of mind. Let them know you have not left their side. Let them know you are mighty you are strong Lord. anything they need you to be you will be. God let them know you love them, and they are not a failure. Lord lift their heads today that they will not walk-in shame. Heal their vision that they see themselves the way that you do. Strengthen them today Lord/Do not let them give up. Give them power to get up. I ask you all this in your son Jesus name.

Amen

ABOUT THE AUTHOR

Love Marie Hobbs is a life changer that uses her words and books to Empower many people to overcome. Love has a famous quote that she lives by. "It is not how you start but how you finish" She is the founder and CEO of Thrifty Styles. A Thriving business that operates globally sending handcrafted crafts all over the world. Love is an Evangelistic Minister that goes around the world spreading the Gospel of Jesus Christ. She is a well-known speaker that travels the world spreading her voice of hope. Love also is a Mentor. She has a mentoring Program C.H.A.N.G.E (Christ Has a Natural Growth Affect).

She is also the Founder of her Upcoming Ministry" Daughters of Zion". In her spare time, she loves to lay on the beach and enjoy the sun. Writing is her passion she has written Six Successful books. Rebirth and "In the Nick of Time" being two of them. If love is not traveling, she enjoys chasing her two grandchildren around that bring her much joy. Love is a mother before anything she is a listener, a friend, a sister.

Here is how you can reach Love:

hobbslove@ymail.com   Instagram: Thrifty Styles

Twitter: Love Hobbs

Facebook: Love Marie Hobbs

Cash app: $Kingskid7777

MINDFUL THOUGHTS

- 36 -

MINDFUL THOUGHTS

MINDFUL THOUGHTS

MINDFUL THOUGHTS